HOW GOOD BOARD MEMBERS BECOME GREAT

BECOME GREAT

FUNDRAISERS

Overcoming the 7 Critical Challenges Volunteers Face

BILL YOUNG

HOW GOOD BOARD MEMBERS BECOME GREAT FUNDRAISERS

Overcoming the 7 Critical Challenges Volunteers Face

Copyright © 2012 Bill Young

Published through Management Factor, Inc. and Printed by Lightning Source/Ingram Content Group. This book was magnificently edited by Sally Young and the excellent interior design provided by Karen Saunders and Kerrie Lian. Incredible cover graphic illustration by Kerrie Lian.

This publication is meant to help your growth and development as a volunteer and/or board member of a nonprofit organization. However, it is not a substitute for advice of your lawyers, accountant, board of directors, government agencies, or any of your advisors, personal or professional.

If you would like more information about webinars, training or additional books, please visit BillYounginspires.com or call 720.221.9214. To order more books click on Bill's Books on the BillYounginspires.com web site.

ISBN 978-0-615-57566-7

Printed in the United States of America

This book has a companion audio recording and webinar as well as in person workshops. In order to get the most benefit from the material, we recommend you read, listen, and attend the online presentation. We all take in information differently depending on our strengths and biases.

We offer special opportunities to attend webinars throughout the year. The introductory webinar is great for new board members and the quarterly webinars and workshops keep the entire team on target.

welcome

THANK YOU FOR PURCHASING THIS BOOK AND FOR ATTENDING the webinar or workshop. You have thousands of choices when it comes to investing in improvement tools and I'm grateful you've chosen this one.

Welcome to a new fundraising world! If you're reading this book it means you currently sit on a board of directors for a nonprofit organization (we use the abbreviated NPO throughout the book), or you are a key volunteer or contemplating taking the plunge to become a board member. Whether you are a veteran Director or new to the field of nonprofit fundraising, you'll face several challenges when you put on your fundraising hat. If you don't have the proper tools you'll soon become demotivated or disgruntled.

I've spent many years in your shoes, watching, listening, and learning how to fundraise. In some cases I've seen what to do and how to do it well and in other cases; I've seen what not to do. I've been instrumental in helping raise multiple millions of dollars in both the nonprofit and for profit fundraising worlds by developing my own fundraising system. Indeed, my experience of helping strategically change the culture and fundraising levels of a very successful volunteer foundation in the Denver area was intense, leading 75 volunteers to increase their fundraising efforts each year. We experienced a new culture, implemented a different leadership style, fostered expanded team goals, and pursued new strategic commitments while raising millions of dollars for hundreds of local children's charities. Our results were dramatic when you consider we raise more funds than foundations 10 or 20 or even 50 times our size.

As a volunteer board member I would estimate that I've spent over 5000 hours offering assistance and consultation on the topic of fundraising. Furthermore, I've read over 100 books on self development, not for profit fundraising, business intelligence, and completed several training courses and workshops in entrepreneurialism. When you add in over 15 years of intense sales and marketing training you'll understand why I'm excited and passionate about what I have to offer in this book. I've read a lot and been trained by some of the best, but the most important part of my experience is real life experience or as they say in the military "real bullets flying." In fact, I have been in the trenches using the strategies in this book to raise money through professional relationships, personal network contacts, and corporate alliances.

How Good Board Members Becomes Great Fundraisers is about taking small steps that lead to large impacts. In our *How Good Become Great Academy* (Fundraising Fire Course), we teach NPO executives, development directors, board members, entrepreneurs, and internal staff to use tools and a system to improve the contributions of each and every person who touches the fundraising activities of their entity. The key is to help them get better, and instead of trying to achieve perfection, to focus them on "improvement over perfection." I've kept this saying in mind during the journey of improving both my internal thoughts and beliefs and external fundraising skills. As you read this book keep the saying in mind, this is your chance for "improvement over perfection."

There are many books on board development and creating effective fundraising campaigns but none focus on the fundraising activities of individual board members and volunteers. This book presents strategies that are simple, customizable, and reproducible. We focus specifically on the day-to-day tasks a board member can implement through their normal life activities to become a great fundraiser. One of the best ways you can help your organization thrive or survive is improve your own skills. Even if you are currently an above average fundraiser, you can get better by learning the strategies in this book.

Good Board Members Can Become Great Fundraisers

Great Fundraisers Create Great Organizations.

Great Organizations Grow and Succeed—Start The FIRE!

About the author

A successful entrepreneur and civic leader, ready to share his expertise

Bill sees himself as an inverse paranoid, convinced that there is a vast conspiracy to make him successful. He has spent his life studying how good become great and now wants to help as many nonprofits and entrepreneurs fulfill their fundraising goals no matter how large or small.

If you're a non-profit leader or business entrepreneur, you may share Bill Young's desire to leave a mark – by bringing revolutionary products or services to market or by improving your community.

Bill has made his mark as an entrepreneur and civic leader. As an entrepreneur, he has raised millions of dollars for companies in his capacity as Board member and owner. As a civic leader, he has raised millions of dollars for children's organizations throughout the Denver area. The Denver Business Journal named Bill to its prestigious Forty Under 40 list and recognized one of his companies, XploreNet, as the sixth Fastest Growing Privately Held Company in Colorado.

Like many successful entrepreneurs, Bill gives back to the community

Deeply committed to improving his community and others' lives, Bill is active in leadership roles in multiple not-for-profit organizations. What motivates him? Helping kids. He believes when you help kids successfully navigate childhood, chances are they'll become responsible adults and ultimately contribute to the community.

During the past decade, Bill has applied the skills that made him a successful businessman to raise funds for non-profits. And countless Denver children have benefited. Bill loves the feeling of being a part of something much bigger than himself. He's proud to contribute to the success of these organizations – and leave his mark on the community.

"An entrepreneur seeks out great ideas … and may be a bit crazy"

"An entrepreneur," says Bill, "must believe so completely in an idea that you'll work around the clock to bring it to fruition. An entrepreneur looks for great ideas or people with great talent, and then finds ways to provide the vision, processes, and money to achieve success."

Bill believes such great ideas can positively impact our lives, and that's why he works so hard to bring them to market. Although he readily admits some might call this crazy, he calls it satisfying.

This book is dedicated to the greatest person I've ever known. And fortunately God chose me to be her husband. The world is a better place because of her and my life would have no value without her.

To my beautiful, amazing Karen. I love you more than words can say.

Table of Contents

introduction

How Good
Board Members
Become Great
Fundraisers

THE WINDS OF CHANGE AND PRESSURES NEVER BEFORE seen are in full force with regard to nonprofit fundraising. Before the recession charitable giving had increased dramatically to a level near $300 Billion in the US in 2006, however, difficult and uncertain times have caused decreases in giving. In fact, according to American Public Media[1], most large charities are expecting a 9% decrease for 2009 and double digit decreases for 2010. Almost a battle like atmosphere has been established which includes people from different political perspectives, small and large businesses and communities attempting to reduce the amount of funding for non-

---

[1] American Public Media Interview 2009)

profit organizations (NPOs) and in some cases, change the way they are taxed or structured. Additional pressure from citizens, politicians, and business leaders to reduce the amount of funding provided to NPOs from government sources and the reality of large cuts to government budgets like Medicare will increase the need for board members to raise more funds. Rest assured that the majority of society still appreciates, approves of, and helps the less fortunate and those who make sacrifices to help those in need.

The green movement, spiritual awaking, and concern over natural resources further demonstrates that society wants to help, but the issue of shifting costs takes center stage when talking about the survival and eventual growth of nonprofits. As a board member of an NPO, whether the organization is a religious group, membership based, trade association, or focused on helping children or the elderly, you have a critical role in deciding whether or not the organization survives the next 24 to 48 months with your own fundraising efforts reshaping and ultimately pushing the organization's mission forward. In order to address cost shifting, you must focus on the donations, sponsorships and in-kind trade that come in via your contacts and behavior. Do not focus on the checks you personally write.

The new economic environment is forcing an already burdened internal NPO staff struggling with less overall funding to try to overcome their number one challenge –fundraising. Indeed, the average size of the Board of Directors for an NPO in the U.S. is 16 voting members[2]. Additional research shows inability to raise money as

---

[2] BoardSource Report 2007, National Center for Nonprofit Boards

the major weakness of most charity boards while only 5% listed fund raising as board strength. Furthermore, board fund raising ranks #1 among areas needing improvement.[3] These statistics demonstrate the pressure on the internal staff members to do less with more, dealing with reduced resources, and the inability to focus on training and maintaining the fundraising efforts of their board. In addition, they have the authority gap, struggling to push and motivate a board that they ultimately work for and are accountable to.

Both internal staff and Board leadership have a few options for overcoming these challenges including increasing the size of their board, using abrasive fear tactics, or connecting their Directors, staff, and volunteers to a third party tool/expert. We've all been involved with the first option which includes adding members and increasing board size to 30, 40, 50 people with the end result of adding more dead weight to the process. Option two tends to lead to disgruntled and de-motivated members because of the abrasive, boiler room culture that is created. Therefore, the best solution is option three, using a third party system, which frees the NPO Executive Officers and Board Chair to focus on other challenges and reduce their workload and stress. This process improves the skills and attitudes of their boards by connecting each Director directly to individualized training. It's time to ignite a blazing fundraising fire and use a third party motivator or "bad cop" (as such), who can deliver consistent tools, motivation, and innovative ideas via webinars, teleseminars, and materials (Books, CDs, Videos, Innovative Tools, etc.)

---

[3] BoardSource Report 2007, National Center for Nonprofit Boards

The ability for you as a board member and the board as a whole to raise critical funds will make or break the organization. According to Boardsource, the "Ten Basic Responsibilities of Nonprofit Boards," were established to help the NPO survive, stay within legal guidelines, and foster successful delivery of services. These responsibilities are easy, straight-forward requirements of any Director; however, fundraising is the most critical initiative for any NPO and typically receives the least amount of focus and training.

The new reality is that everyone has to do more with less and although entities will run, hide or quit during these challenging and changing times, others will rise above the rest, raising more money than ever before while establishing new records in the process. This requires many types of changes including new attitudes, vocabulary, beliefs, and behavior. The fundraising world is transforming at the speed of light with new challenges and new opportunities connecting, but if you don't change the culture of your board then you'll continue to do what you've always done. In fact, as the new attitude and movement over the next five to ten years may provide, there seem to be three different approaches to fundraising.

1. Good fundraising boards become great ones through use of a third party innovative training system [IDEAL]

2. Traditional boards keep doing things the way they always have done and hope that they stay in business [TYPICAL RESPONSE]

3. Boards that are out of business (probably don't know it yet) rely on the government contracts or someone else to figure it out for them [NOT EFFECTIVE]

Board Members are first and foremost Fundraisers and have three options:

1. Write checks yourself
2. Find others to write checks
3. Find resources and relationships that turn into value

According to BoardSouce, only about 40 percent of charity board members feel comfortable asking other people to donate to their organizations. It is assumed that you'll donate yourself and according to the same source, 75 percent of you do, besides it is almost required that you personally give some type of funds. However, the opportunity lies within this book, focusing on #2 and #3 and providing a road map for individuals to find more people to write checks; increasing the number of relationships they have that can bring additional value to the organization.

Whether you use traditional funding processes or new cultivation models, you still need to get people into the circles, path ways, and flow charts. In fact, when it comes to actual day-to-day follow through many challenges tend to surface such as; lack of training, process, time, and focus. Furthermore, new approaches, tools and a shift in paradigms are required to counter the outdated methods. There are too many people asking for money using the wrong approaches and tools. It is not about just asking for money, but rather letting the process and tools do the asking and inviting for you, customized to your time schedule, personality, and style. Both experienced and new board members need new strategies to overcome the seven challenges outlined in this book, increasing both the volume of sponsors and number of donors.

Many board members become great leaders, but the fundraising part seems to elude them. Their passion and desire to help is second to none and with a full head of steam they press forward to make a difference, sacrificing time and resources. They provide the organization with experience, labor, and passion. The lack of proper knowledge and a system leaves only experience, trial and error, and personal motivation to guide them. The reality is that great fundraisers see the past as a resource, they are committed in the now, and they are willing to tackle the future. In the end, they realize that if they do not bring their best efforts to the entity whether it is for six months, one year or five years, the entity will cease to exist. They need the seven strategies presented later in the book to help their NPO succeed, going from good to great in the process. These strategies are built on the core pillars of the acronym POWER.

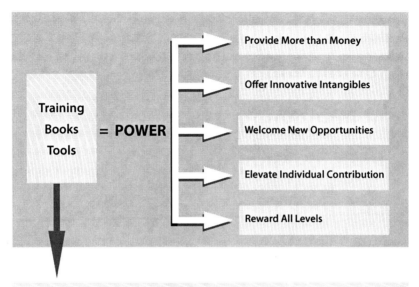

Training
Books = POWER
Tools

Provide More than Money

Offer Innovative Intangibles

Welcome New Opportunities

Elevate Individual Contribution

Reward All Levels

How Good Board Members Become Great Fundraisers Webinars and Workshops are held on a quarterly basis and productive for both new members to your board or to help your veterans stay on target throughout the year.

Many of the ideas and concepts expressed in this book you've heard before however you will also learn new tactics and techniques that if implemented, will improve your efforts by 10%, 50% and in some cases 1000%. Before we get into specific tactics that you can incorporate we'll cover the seven challenges in detail which are called assumptions in this book because we're assuming you've experienced them in the past or are facing similar ones now. In fact, these seven challenges incapacitate 95% of the NPO industry's fundraising efforts. The inability for most organizations' to confront or even know the challenges points to why so many organizations report that fundraising efforts are falling well below their expectations and their current and past board members are disgruntled. For you to start "improvement over perfection", you need to start with assumption number one, the **NPO Time Trap**.

I: The NPO Time Trap

YOU ARE KIND, HEART-FELT, HELPFUL, CONSISTENT, impressive, loving, giving, respectful, committed, and positive. In addition, according to the Booze Allen Company[4], the research shows that you're close to 50 years old (the range is 34 — 64), above average income and intelligence, college educated, score high on the empathy scale, and have a difficult time saying no. One of the challenges you inevitably find yourself confronted with is too much to do and not enough time to do it. This is not an uncommon problem, intending to make a difference and finding that your smack dab in middle of the Nonprofit Organizational time trap. You're looking for

---

[4] Booze Allen 2005 Research Study

ways to increase your personal contributions, but the options must fit your personal lifestyle. Volunteer work should help your growth, not incapacitate your priorities and responsibilities. Your attitude and motivation often suffer in response to this situation.

In today's fast paced society we're all trying to do more in less time while attempting to balance family and personal life with professional commitments. Technology has only complicated this balancing act since we can text, twit, post, and call from anywhere to just about every place on the globe. Your challenges increase when you add nonprofit activities to your life. You joined the board to provide assistance, improve your skills, learn more about the community, meet like-minded people, and RAISE FUNDS! However, your number one priority is your family, friends, and other personal interests and time with them is critical and important. Furthermore, you have critical career development objectives like increasing income, knowledge, and opportunities. You are committed to both time and resources necessary to fulfill these objectives, however, in order to provide value you'll need to dedicate more time to fundraising. You quickly find yourself in the trap, pushing forward without the awareness of unique time management tools to help you break free.

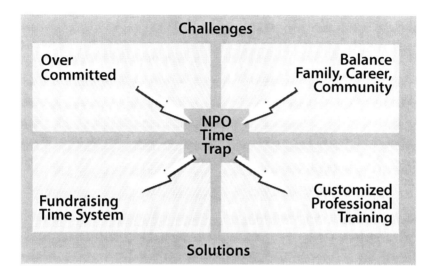

You only add to the challenge when you agree to serve on additional boards. Once you've served on one you become a target for others. They approach you to bring value to their mission so you find yourself sitting on two, three, five, 10 or more boards. The responsibility of raising funds for each can become overwhelming and soon you find yourself writing resignation letters or worst yet going MIA (Missing in Action).

Research conducted by Boardsource[5] reflects that the average board member spends 10 hours per month on Board/committee business. This breaks down to 2.5 hours per week or 30 minutes per work day. If thirty minutes is the average then we must assume the range is five minutes to one hour. This data reflects that you have very little time to accomplish key tasks and when considering that most people lack good time management skills, escaping the trap becomes close to impossible. Plus, ac-

---

[5] BoardSource Report 2007, National Center for Nonprofit Boards

cording to David Lewis in a Boston Globe[6] article; 43% of Americans categorize themselves as disorganized with 21% having missed vital work deadlines. Nearly half say disorganization causes them to work late at least two or more times each week. Therefore, even when you do find the extra minutes to work on fundraising tasks you may struggle with how to organize the time in the most efficient manner. The key issue isn't sacrificing more time, but to paraphrase Brian Tracey, you have to eliminate unimportant tasks and focus on priorities.

This trap demands a new game plan, utilizing time management techniques and tools customized for board members like the FUNDRAISING TIME MANAGEMENT SYSTEM (Strategy 2) and extending your professional activities. You cannot expand your day to more than 24 hours, but you can manage your commitment and tasks differently and move on to breaking through the next assumption, **The Knowledge Ceiling**.

---

[6] Boston Globe 3/12/06 Esselte survey, David Lewis

assumption

2: The Knowledge Ceiling

YOU DON'T HAVE A BACHELOR DEGREE IN FUNDRAISING and your current experience only helps you grow to a certain level. NPOs need board members and volunteers to jump in and start helping right from the start. However, most do not have the time or tools to properly educate you. Their intentions are good, but their options are limited. Your knowledge about fundraising is limited so you end up caught in a cycle of either using ineffective outdated behaviors or failure via trial and error. This circumstance makes you hit the ceiling very quickly. As the cycle continues, you become more frustrated often losing your motivation and in the end reducing your contribution level. Even if you've been a board member for 20 years, expanding your fundraising knowledge will significantly help bring in more sponsorships and donors.

You are a volunteer and like all volunteers you can only carry out what you are instructed to do. The instruction you receive is not always focused on fundraising techniques, but includes other vital topics like governance, strategic plans, satisfaction surveys, and meeting minutes. Although these are important areas to cover, developing your knowledge and techniques should have a high priority. Plus, your executive leadership is already overloaded with internal fundraising goals and challenges and they do not have the time to inspire or the authority to properly implement and to reinforce. Indeed, they often feel embarrassed or frustrated from playing the bad cop when the board falls short. As a result, you end up trying to improve your skills by playing the "guessing game", watching the activities and style of other board members and volunteers, with no idea as to which ones are strong or weak fundraisers. If you're lucky you model after someone who is really good, but for the most part you tend to pick up bad habits or worse no habits at all.

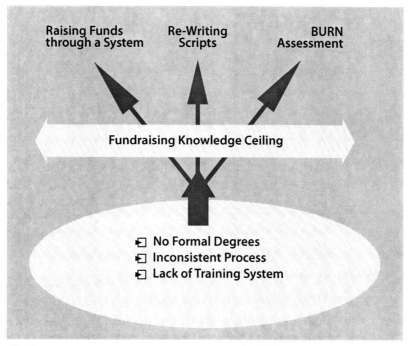

The lack of board member assessment tools like our BURN AS-SESSMENT© (Strategy 1) puts you at a disadvantage from the start. Most organizations give it their best effort to assess a new member's potential contribution, but lack the right tools to complete the process. You often end up working on the wrong challenges or as the saying goes, "doing the same thing over and over and expecting something different." Once you know your strengths, you can address how to make them stronger while making a game plan for avoiding identified weaknesses. A good assessment creates a starting point of confidence and builds skills and knowledge that help you deliver results. You avoid the trauma caused by improperly approaching people making the process comfortable for both you and them. Often times it is not your effort that is lacking but your understanding of the fundraising process that needs improvement.

Many assumptions are made about your fundraising knowledge including your ability to establish proper personal goals, organize your daily/weekly efforts, and change ineffective behaviors simply because you come from a professional background. The internal staff assumes that you know how to invite, ask, or foster your relationships. You've spent time in the trenches of a professional field developing great experience in strategic planning, operations, sales, accounting, law, marketing, entrepreneurship, and leadership. However, offering sponsorships and cultivating donors is a different type of animal requiring different knowledge, time division, and innovative approaches.

Whether you are a new or veteran board member, learning the right information provides fall-back support when you run into the usual roadblocks. This knowledge system must be consistent, taught from day one, and simple, producing new opportunities, changing negative scripts, and helping you rectify assumption #3 **Negative Experiences** of past efforts.

3: Negative Experiences

YOU HAVE EXPERIENCED THE BAD AND THE UGLY ESPECIALLY when you watched the Board Chair or internal staff (ED, DO, FO, etc.) uncomfortably push, probe, and unfortunately in some situations, abrasively direct the board to raise more money. At times you've felt the emotional vale in the room going back and forth from the quiet of a pin drop to the brink of uncomfortable laughter, ready to explode into anger at any moment. You sat there either confused by the process or you took the initiative and overcame these issues on your own, bringing in lots of sponsors, donors, and resources. Furthermore, your negative experience was compounded when you brought in lots of value only to watch other board members not contribute. This entire fundraising dance left you feeling overwhelmed and isolated.

On the other hand, your organization's culture dictated that the topic of board fundraising either be covered as quickly as possible or never mentioned at all. The tone was almost apologetic or uncomfortable, an afterthought buried in the bottom of a letter. If this is your first experience, then you're lucky because you have not witnessed this dance yet. The organizations that create a fun proactive fundraising culture through innovative ideas are few and far between while entities that struggle with this topic end up building the foundation for your next negative experience.

Board meeting formats often add to the frustration. Most board agendas tend to fall in other categories even though fundraising was identified in the research as the greatest challenge for board members. The two to four hour meetings entail well planned, quality agendas with the leadership attempting to talk about fundraising without beating a dead horse or getting on a soapbox. Unfortunately there is not enough time to work one on one with each member on individual fundraising efforts and the lack of effective tools used leaves members feeling isolated, trying to raise funds with only their recent negative experience guiding them. New models like cultivation modeling and donor flow take some of this pressure off; however, getting the prospective sponsor or donor into the model is still a major challenge. You still have to ask or invite and if you do these tasks poorly you'll be left feeling embarrassed or guilty from letting down the rest of the team.

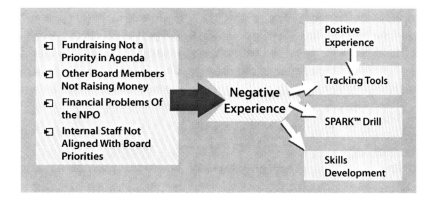

Your frustration can grow from not knowing where you stand to not knowing if you are improving or failing. Most organizations do not appropriately track the funding process; leaving them unable to track the contribution of each member other than the direct dollars they give. There may be members helping contribute $50 while the efforts of some may equal $50,000. The NPO is unable to verify and then unable to capitalize on what could be working well and discontinue ineffective steps. If you do not measure or track fundraising activities (individual as well as cumulative), then do not do these activities. You will struggle with making corrections if you are unable to identify the problems or opportunities. This process isn't used to put uncomfortable attention on people or pat people on the back, but used to provide assistance to those who need it. In fact, tracking contribution helps leaders change their culture and create positive experiences for the board.

When reviewed as a direct component, individual board member fundraising pales in comparison to other funding channels like corporate giving, foundation grants, and government contracts, however, creating a positive experience and growing SuperStars© can become the organizations most important success factor. Positive, enthusiastic people who are properly trained open doors to relationships in all the above channels. When you develop a positive fundraising culture, you dramatically improve the financial performance of the organization through the boards' circle of influence and community ties.

Great fundraisers help create this positive fundraising culture, improving the internal staff's efforts and motivation, fostering new relationships and expanding the momentum of the team. During the learning phase, they put away the baggage of negative experiences and focus on making changes to both their attitude and ability to help. In the end, your negative experience from not contributing can cause the organization to end up missing financial goals. You do not bring in the necessary money, resources, and/or in-kind trade to keep the NPO on course. Again, the goal is for each board member to bring in value not directly from their own check book, but through their network, professional relationships, personal hobbies, and day-to-day activities. This is accomplished when the members feel positive, confident, and comfortable. One of the most fundamental ways to provide great experiences is to understand and overcome assumption #4, **The Borrower Phenomenon**.

4: The Borrower Phenomenon

YOU TIGHTEN UP WHILE THINKING ABOUT ASKING OTHERS FOR money or inviting them to attend a cultivation event or send in their sponsorship agreement because you have mental scripts playing in your head often without your conscious awareness. For some, the reluctance to invite or ask is caused by weak time management skills or the lack of proper techniques, but in most cases your mental scripts are stalling your efforts.

These scripts deal with all kinds of categories including human interaction, ego issues, intelligence, and personal expectations, with the most well established ones surrounding money. Money scripts are often thick and ingrained starting in early childhood and fostered into young adulthood. You may not realize that you are caught in the Borrower Phenomenon©. Most people are not aware of the power or influence of these scripts until they stop, sit down and think about it. However once they do; they start to realize the importance of overcoming this phenomenon. The affects of the phenomenon often overpowers your desire to take appropriate action and suffocates the board with delusion. It reduces quality behavior even if your well trained and decreases the likelihood of accomplishing major fundraising goals.

When you go to a movie you experience a real life example of the power of mental scripts. For example, have you ever cried while attending a movie or become intensely scared? Excited and motivated? You knew the movie was not real yet the script, the characters and the flow made you feel something. The entire process worked all your senses and made you feel like what you were seeing on the screen was real. Go ahead and stand up in the theatre and go touch the screen, look behind it and you'll see that it is just equipment, a wall with no boogeyman or hero standing there. Your mind cannot differ between what was vividly imagined and what was real for the two hours you sat in front of the screen. Similar to a movie, your mental scripts cause you to react in certain ways; often times in ways that do not benefit your actions and are illogical or outside of reality. All the mental scripts you've picked up along the way cause your fundraising efforts to feel more like begging which is more a subconscious effect than a conscious one. You go back and forth in your mind between asking for too much or too little which can cause fear and embarrassment. The challenges get greater when you realize the contradictory fundraising scripts of the entire organization and fellow members.

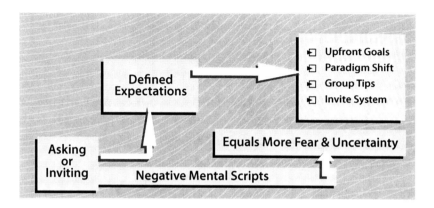

If you're in doubt regarding this phenomenon, then ask a fellow board member questions such as: "What is a lot of money for us to fundraise either individually or as a board?" "How much money should the entire NPO raise this year?" Or, "What is the individual fundraising goal of each board member?" To the last question, you'll hear answers ranging from $500 to $50,000 and depending on the answer, the amounts create the script for everyone to follow. In most cases the difference between raising $5,000 and $5,000,000 is the current expectation not the reality of available funds or resources.

The overall board expectations are tied to the personal scripts of each member. In fact, the entire group can either lower the bar or raise it depending on their individual beliefs. Unfortunately, the internal staff often creates these initial money scripts and they're often based on personal issues or negative past results. In fact, if you are a veteran to the fundraising game, then you've seen this affect when you were indoctrinated into the "we only raise so much money," script. The reality is that until the board members understand the roadblocks caused by their own scripts, taking the step to increase the goals is pointless.

The Borrower Phenomenon is similar to watching a homeless person ask for money and it affects many areas of your organization including day-to-day operations, goal setting, and sponsorship structures. The same type of mental script as observing a homeless person solicit money from strangers begins to play in the board member's mind. They begin to feel unfortunate, lost, confused, or overbearing. They wonder within if the person they've approached will frown upon them for asking for their attendance or asking to give a personal donation. These feelings have nothing to do with the person's real psyche or with the importance of actually asking people for assistance, but naturally appear when they are put in the uncomfortable position of asking for anything relating to money. Even if you are an exception you still deal with strong money scripts.

Money scripts fall into three main areas including the amount of money considered to be a lot of money, where the money comes from, and the way in which it is obtained. These scripts are mostly subconscious, but can be addressed with new ones written at the conscious level. Money scripts come from many sources including family, friends, jobs, community organizations, school, and media. Your parents probably created some of the strongest scripts when they said, "little one, you never ask other people for money – it's rude." They had positive intentions however they caused you a life time of issues when it comes to fundraising. More specifically, with your volunteer time the scripts can be even stronger because no one is making a profit off what you are doing and it can be looked at as bothering (or begging) others just by inviting them to help. As a board member, you must be assertive when asking for established fundraising goals for each member and open dialogue about money scripts. You can use parts of your SPARK© DRILL (Strategy 7) to discuss and re-write these scripts. Overcoming these "old ways of thinking" can have a positive impact on your efforts when dealing with assumption #5 – **Inefficient Personal Network**.

5: Inefficient Personal Network

YOU ARE UNABLE TO FUNDRAISE AT THE LEVEL YOU WOULD LIKE because your existing network is not large enough, lacks strength and depth and is not expanding fast enough. Furthermore, your front line contacts have a reduction in their circle of influence or you've saturated them. You may have the misperception that everyone is getting hit up by everyone, everywhere. You could be struggling with utilizing the proper way to make a new contact or even worse you are committing one of the seven deadly sins of networking. Now add to this situation that you lack the initiative to go to new events or upon arrival the fear of creating new contacts is paralyzing. Even though most of us are overwhelmed with our existing nonprofit commitments, good techniques and practices still foster great relationships. People want to help you. You want to avoid becoming just another person in their network demanding something from them, either time or money, and begin to realize the inefficiency of your current personal network.

Over the last few years networking has become a hot topic and overused buzz word. Most people only think about networking when they need something; a new job, a new project, a new customer or a new sponsor. They try to meet as many people as possible often losing connections to their close relationships. They tend to focus on the volume of connections on LinkedIn or Face book rather the quality of the people they are interacting with on a daily basis. The networking game definitely involves the volume of people but if you play correctly you will strengthen your existing relationships and systematically expand your professional network. However, if you misjudge internal and external politics along with the priorities of each person that comes in contact with you, then you will miss out on the opportunity to improve the mining of your current network and expand it with new quality contacts.

There are many misconceptions about reaching out to your current network to educate and have them donate to your organization. These include: "I tried it and it didn't work." "It's exploiting others." "I don't know how to talk to people." "Just use the cultivation system." "I just need to give them material," "The NPO provided me with a script," or the most popular one, "They're getting asked by everyone." All of these assumptions or reactions cause you to write off your existing network and avoid approaching them all together. The key challenge has to do with how you ask rather than if you ask. You need to use tools and a process that provides value to them always remembering the importance of WIFT (What's in it for them).

Board members are unable to raise funds through their network due to three key issues. The first issue is skill level; struggling with techniques to properly ask or invite donations and sponsorships. Building relationships is a skill and just like any other skill you must learn the intricacies and then practice the techniques. The second challenge is attitude; falling down from having a poor mind set about soliciting your network. You go into the interaction anticipating the worst, letting your biases guide your behavior resulting with a poor taste in the mouth for both you and the contact. The third major issue is lack of strategy, causing you to overlook key steps in the process and lose motivation from confusion and struggle. You are not sure which step your currently working on or which one is next in the process.

The challenge expands when the NPO staff attempts to work with a board member to help farm their network correctly. They are doing their best, offering specific tools that help engage but not enrage the members of the network. They often give you letters or material and then suggest that you write down a list of everyone you know. They insist that you send an e-mail or pick up the phone and start dialing. Many people assume that because your contact knows you they will help. The fundamental change here is treating everyone like a customer and under promise and over deliver. You often commit one of the sins of networking by your inability to offer your contacts value causing frustration when most of them do not provide assistance to your organization.

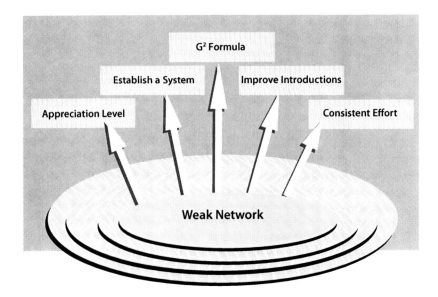

The seven deadly sins of networking are lack of gratitude, getting before you give, sporadic efforts, failing the trust step, providing weak introductions, mismatching people, and passing the buck.

1. *Lack of Gratitude:* Many people fail to show their appreciation for help extended to them and overlook the fact that everyone in your network likes appreciation. They miss opportunities to send hand-written thank you notes or value e-mails that have special meaning to their contact.

2. *Getting Before You Give:* They often try to get before they give, becoming a taker expecting help right away. They often wait to give value until the other person has made the first move or went out of their way to offer assistance.

3. *Sporadic Efforts:* Their efforts are often sporadic, attending events only during the holidays or in the summer time. Networking is a continuous process

where people get to see you several times, at several functions, becoming comfortable with your style and goals.

4. *Failing the Trust Step:* They often forget to follow up or follow through on any commitments they made. Building trust is about displaying GENU-INE CREDIBILITY© (Strategy 4).

5. *Providing Weak Introductions:* They rush through trying to connect people without giving the right specifics or properly setting up the rules of engagement.

6. *Mismatching People:* They are unable to articulate why two people should meet or they have such a weak understanding of each person's strengths that they overlook connection points.

7. *Passing the Buck:* They expect others to do the work for them, passing along portfolio, services or bio information and then sitting back and waiting for the introductions to come in. They overestimate others desire and focus to help them accomplish their goals.

Whether you have 15 minutes a week or 15 hours, you can become a more effective board member by evaluating your network properly, establishing a referral and introduction system, improving the quality of introductions and following through on a consistent basis. The key is to have a system that is easily understood, takes a short time frame to get up to speed, and gets you the results both you and the NPO expect. If you're properly working your network and avoiding the seven deadly sins, then you will be increasing your level of contribution; however, you can end up with unintended consequences or caught in **The Giving Trap** which is the next assumption.

6: The Giving Trap

YOU BECOME EXCITED AND MOTIVATED ABOUT RAISING MONEY, pouring over your contact list, address book, Christmas card inventory, and outlook database identifying who would be good to approach. You've learned new processes and techniques for expanding your network and elevating your contribution. Your prospect list is a critical step in your efforts but often puts you on the path to falling into The Giving Trap©. This trap is built on great intention but marred with potential land mines. Everyone you put on your list using your Superstar Tool© can and will become donors and sponsors for your NPO. They gratefully give both money and time signing up their company to sponsor your event or even donating loads of their own cash to you. This sounds great and is exactly what you were targeting, however, now the trap grabs hold of you.

Reciprocal giving is a major part of the fundraising game. If they attend your event, then you'll be expected to attend their event. Another example is if you send an e-mail to Jane Doe asking for a donation, there is a good chance Jane will be asking you for one. This puts you in a tough position unless you have the budget to give to 100 or even a 1000 different organizations depending on the size of your network. You'll end up going broke or becoming so busy you'll lose your job. You do want to reciprocate, following the G2 FORMULA© (Strategy 5); however, if not done properly you'll soon be overburdened with excessive time and financial commitments. The challenge of getting out of the giving trap is often one of the biggest challenges that you will face when you try to contribute as a board member.

As mentioned in the introduction, nearly $300 billion was given to NPOs in 2006 with a marked decrease expected in 2009 and 2010. The overall macro view may be down, but individual giving has been and will continue to be up. People want to help you, but they expect you to help them in return. In fact, volunteering and giving remain a part of the philanthropic efforts of most individuals. A Bank of American study (Bank Of America High Net Worth Study, 2007) reflects that on average people volunteered 241 hours in 2007. The results showed that the more hours a person volunteered the more money they gave. This study not only proves that people are still giving but it also reflects the opportunity you have to push your contacts to give more time and resources as well as their money. And in the end, they may end up giving more money than you originally thought. As the economy turns around, people will look for ways to help out their local community. They often don't give because they have their own financial commitments or they do not perceive an alternative way to reciprocate other than writing you a check. They can help you and you can help them without any money changing hands but there must be different options and structured alternatives for reciprocal giving.

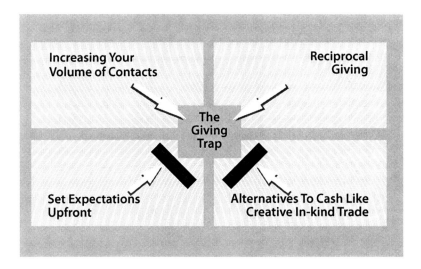

There are several strategies for avoiding this trap including: becoming a resource center for your network, providing lots of value with little financial commitment, making yourself a talent scout to find people in your network who can help each other, and providing honest feedback and upfront agreements to those who are willing and able to provide you with donations and sponsorship dollars. If you are authentic, offering creative alternatives to cash for your contacts, then you can succeed. If you're fortunate enough to avoid the giving trap then you may find yourself frustrated due to assumption 7 – **Absence of a System**.

7. Absence of a System

YOU SHOW UP TO BOARD MEETINGS OR RECEIVE E-MAILS WITH the dialog or content pushing you to fundraise. You ask yourself, "Where do I start?" Indeed, you'll receive brochures and flyers along with heart tugging stories and lively case studies. Now, the pressure is on you to go out and make it happen. The key analysis here is for you to understand why the results do not match the intent. There are only three reasons you do not raise money, either you don't want to, you're not told up front of this expectation, or there resonates a lack of process to follow. If the reason is you do not want to do it or you're too busy, you have to evaluate why you're on the board. If you're willing and the results are not coming from your actions, then you need a proven system to follow.

The main challenge with each board's process is that it ends up looking like the common training approach called "passing it along" process or "the secret circle".

The secret circle is the situation where key information is transferred from one person to the next. One person attempts to train or teach a system to the next person, similar to telling a secret, and that person passes the secret on to the next person and on and on (1 to 2 to 3, etc. in diagrams below). In the diagram titled Typical Information Distortion, the secret is nothing like the original by the time it gets around to the person who started the circle. This is similar to the fundraising skills and goals of most NPOs. The recipient takes in the information taught to them by a fellow board member, attempts to translate it (see change in shape with each person) and then passes it along to the next person. Each person in the circle gives it their best effort to listen, interpret, and then teach. The problem is that with each transfer information is lost and distorted. At this point, you have one hand tied behind your back before you even go out to raise the first dollar.

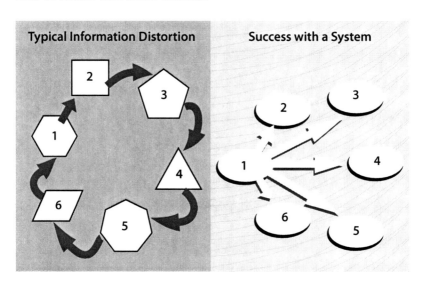

This circle with distorted shapes shows how information gets changed and a new version is created with each person. The end result is that members have the passion and drive to help, but lack a sound, tested, and consistent system taught by one person or information coming from one source as reflected in the Success with a System diagram. The NPO ends up underutilizing abilities and missing key goals. In fact, many members become confused, frustrated, and de-motivated.

The Success with a System diagram demonstrates how everyone learns the same process and information. The training is consistent, credible, and cutting edge, enabling board members to focus on fundraising activities rather than wasting time trying to teach and train others.

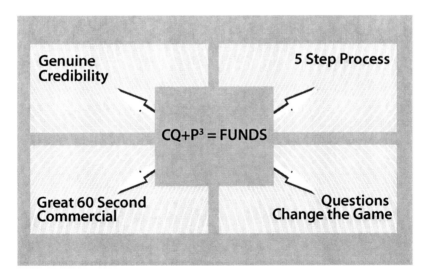

The world of fundraising has changed similar to every other industry – there are better ways to receive donations, sponsorships, and in-kind contributions. Similar to improvements in technology, materials, and teaching, fundraising systems have evolved. Today it is more important than ever to follow steps that lead to long term success. Besides, you are offering something less tangible than a house, car, technology, etc. You are a volunteer and only have a few hours each week to provide value so if you're stumbling through without a process, attempting to learn from ill prepared fellow volunteers, then you're wasting what little time you have to help. You don't need, nor do you have the time, to learn a complex way to bring in funds. Therefore, your team must use simple tools like the SPARK DRILL™ (Strategy 7) to clearly define the organization's fundraising expectations, to create a fantastic 60 second commercial, to offer consistent reinforcement, and to improve each person's level of contribution.

Board Power System

I'VE MADE ASSUMPTIONS IN THE PRIOR SECTION REGARDING the challenges you may face, but now we'll do some quick assessments to determine your starting point. As the short story below illustrates (Forwarded from a friend of mine named Richard), you can get in trouble when you make assumptions.

The ASSumption Story

His request approved, the CNN News photographer quickly used a cell phone to call the local airport to charter a flight. He was told a twin-engine plane would be waiting for him at the airport. Arriving at the airfield, he spotted a plane warming up outside a hanger.

He jumped in with his bag, slammed the door shut, and shouted, "Let's go". The pilot taxied out, swung the plane into the wind and took off. Once in the air, the photographer instructed the pilot, 'Fly over the valley and make low passes so I can take pictures of the fires on the hillsides. "Why?" asked the pilot.

"Because I'm a photographer for CNN', he responded, and I need to get some close up shots." The pilot was strangely silent for a moment, finally he stammered, "So, what you're telling me, is . . . You're NOT MY FLIGHT INSTRUCTOR?"

"Life is short - ASK A LOT OF GOOD QUESTIONS."

How Great Board Members Become Great Fundraisers includes seven strategies with over 25 tactics incorporated, that when implemented will improve your POWER as a board member. This is POWER you bring to the fundraising efforts of the entire NPO. If you have identified with the one or more of the assumed challenges that most if not all Board Members and volunteers face, then you can start to make the transition from good to great. This transformation is not easy, but it is obtainable and is about IMPROVEMENT OVER PERFECTION©.

The strategies are built off of the five pillars of POWER, incorporate real world activities, simple changes, and innovative thinking and include concepts, solutions, and tactics that will improve your individual contribution and in the end help the organization hit major goals and exceed expectations.

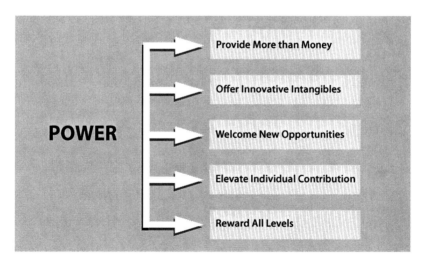

Let's take the POWER Assessment. Read through each sentence and then check off rarely, sometimes or always and at the end count how many times you checked always.

1. I ask my prospective donor/sponsor about their charities and passions before I talk about mine

   Rarely ___   Sometimes ___   Always ___

2. I customize my 60 second commercial depending on who I am talking with

   Rarely ___   Sometimes ___   Always ___

3. I block out 30 minutes per week to just do fundraising activities

   Rarely ___   Sometimes ___   Always ___

4. I write out my personal goals each week and then connect them to the NPO goals

   Rarely ___   Sometimes ___   Always ___

5. The NPO helps me establish my personal fundraising goals at the start of the year

   Rarely ___   Sometimes ___   Always ___

6. I feel professional and comfortable when I'm asking for a sponsorship or in-kind trade

   Rarely ___   Sometimes ___   Always ___

7. I use a tickler system to help me invite contacts to participate in cultivation models

   Rarely ___   Sometimes ___   Always ___

8. I use the two to three pain points that my NPO solves during discussions about the organization

   Rarely ___   Sometimes ___   Always ___

9. I offer my network more than donations to avoid the giving trap

   Rarely ___   Sometimes ___   Always ___

10. Our NPO completes a quick fundraising exercise during our board and committee meetings

    Rarely ___   Sometimes ___   Always ___

POWER is about expanding your influence and creating new fundraising results for the organization.

P P stands for Provide More Than Money. Even though your number one priority as a board member is to provide funding to the NPO whether directly from you or another source, the NPO needs you to provide more than money in order to make changes and accomplish more significant milestones. This value is critical, often hard to define, and makes the difference between success and failure. Through self analysis, simple changes, and authenticity, you will begin to manage time differently, create positive case studies, and re-write old money scripts. We need to understand, and if necessary, change your mind set about fundraising.

O O stands for Offering Innovative Intangibles. An intangible is not always clear to define or perceived by the sense of touch. These are things that often cannot be picked up or they may be hard to value. In fact, in order to get your arms around it, you may have to see how your individual efforts connect to the overall mission and fundraising goals. Examples of intangibles include customer good will, aesthetic appeal or team morale. For our purposes, we'll use the term to mean steps you can take or gifts you can offer that go beyond tangible items such as dollars and checks. The reality is that if you can master the things not seen or held, you can often reach new, increased fundraising goals. Furthermore, intangibles take on a more difficult process when expressing them in an individual or board structure and understanding which ones affect performance. They are often identified with a board's overall results whether they are positive or negative. The NPO you represent is looking for you to offer more in the way of collaboration, knowledge, processes, and relationships, but they can't always articulate their needs or how to put you on the path to production/reaching those goals. Great training can do this.

W W stands for Welcome New Opportunities. When you welcome new opportunities, you set the stage for growth and development of new revenue channels. Who have you not contacted to ask for funds? According to Boardsource, only 40% of the board members in the country are comfortable with asking for donations. They are often uncomfortable because they haven't been taught how to properly ask or they continue to go down the same road. In fact, members often farm the same list and people and the natural progression is for that list to get smaller and smaller every six months. We're defining unique as the only one or the sole example, leading to the improbable. You may have opportunities that have are unparallel to previous efforts whether they be people you have not talked to about your NPO or resources you've overlooked. There are individual contribution results waiting for you to accomplish.

 E stands for Elevate. We are often asked to take our contributions to the "next level" but next level means different things to different people. The key here is to focus on small shifts keeping in mind the value of improvement over perfection. Evaluate the details of what is being asked of you and if you understand the NPOs expectations. If you do then you can start to elevate your own contributions. Elevate means to rise to a higher place or state, promoting the overall fundraising objectives not once a month or quarter, but in every interaction. This is not about being a cheerleader, but rather using enthusiasm and tools to motivate yourself and your fellow board members to raise the bar, expect something better, and know that they have support and resources to fall back on.

R R stands for Reward All Levels. Donors, sponsors, cheerleaders and superstars love appreciation and while some like cash and prizes others go for fame and portfolio bullet points. The key here is to reward everyone at every level. It is often as simple as saying thank you or sending a hand written note each and every time there is an opportunity. In other cases, you may need to send a gift certificate or tickets to an event. Either way, you must connect to every contact that helps or even attempts to help the NPO. To further state this point, appreciate and thank everyone all the time, every minute, every second. This is a simple concept, but overlooked again and again.

strategy

1: Personal Alignment

THE FOUNDATION OF SUCCESSFUL FUNDRAISING COMES down to aligning your personal passion and goals with those of the organization. In fact, most people are unaware of any misalignment between the organizations goals, values and beliefs until a later point in the relationship. You typically get involved via either a personal relationship with an internal staff or fellow board member or you receive services directly from the organization. You simply do not think about the connection until you've already made your commitment and you're sitting in a board or committee meeting offering your contribution.

Alignment is the connection you make between the key objectives of the NPO and your own and includes understanding your rights, obligations, other member's values, and expected activities. Most research shows that organizations fail because there is not an alignment between the previous mentioned issues and the board member or volunteer. For example, if you've had a negative experience with fundraising, then you either bring that baggage with you or try to forget that it ever happened. The past problems that lead to your frustration could exist with the new organization so correcting those issues should not be underestimated.

On the other hand, you may have had total control of decision making, directional strategy, and tactical plans in your other roles, but find yourself sitting on the bench with the NPO. Understanding the expectations on you and being on the same page with the new internal staff makes the entire process fun and easy. You avoid the borrower phenomenon and achieve alignment when you know your own strengths and wiring along with your personal goals and beliefs. This connects your behavior to key results and raises your motivation. Lastly, your commitment level is solidified when your personal vision is aligned with mission of the NPO.

Great fundraisers complete some simple self analysis steps including evaluating their own ability to listen, analyze opportunities, think clearly and creatively, work well with others and lead by example. They're willing to prepare for key meetings, ask the right questions of prospective donors and sponsors, contribute resources, open the right doors, and develop and improve fundraising skills that they may not currently posses. If you properly assess your personal strengths and fundraising abilities, establish written goals, evaluate current beliefs, then you can choose the appropriate options for helping.

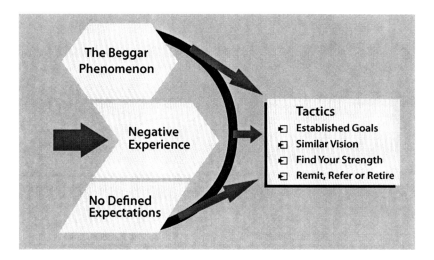

Find Your Strength

The famous Greek Delphi site had the words, "Know thyself," inscribed on the Temple of Apollo. Even the Latin version of this original thought is written on a plaque above the Oracle's door in the Matrix film series. The point is; in order to evaluate and help others, you have to understand your own strengths and figure out the methods to making them stronger. You say fundraising is one of your weaknesses, but do you understand the reasons why you're struggling or is it after completing a self assessment you find that fundraising is a strength? If we're going to improve your fundraising skills we need to find out what you're good at and which areas cause you to struggle. This is where self analysis plays a key part in the process. If you understand your own wiring, you'll begin to understand the wiring of your prospective donors/sponsors, increasing the donations and help they provide.

The first step is to purchase the **Strengthfinder 2.0 book** (http://strengths.gallup.com) and take the strength assessment. Both the Wall Street Journal and USA Today listed this book as a best seller. It takes about 20 minutes to complete the assessment and you'll appreciate the results, helping you start the process of identifying why you may not be raising money for your NPO. They spent several years researching how people can identify their own talents and as the Strengthfinder system describes their process with a question, "Do you have the opportunity to do what you do best *every day*?" The book points out that, "All too often, our natural talents go untapped. From the cradle to the cubicle, we devote more time to fixing our shortcomings than to developing our strengths." The tool adds additional value by uncovering your talents to find out why you're struggling with certain tasks.

Another great self analysis tool is the DISC tool offered through several sales and management consulting firms. DISC® is a personality assessment that helps you better understand your own wring along with your strengths and challenges of your behavior. You must use a credible tool to find out your strengths so that you can start to identify new options to achieve new fundraising opportunities.

BURN ASSESSMENT©
The NFL has the combines and the Olympics have the trials to determine the athletes starting point, ranking to others, and likely hood of organizational fit. We use the BURN assessment to help the board evaluate the fundraising skills and personal alignment of their existing and new members.

BURN is an acronym meaning:
Current **B**eliefs
& **U**nderstanding **R**esponses
Nurtures behavior

This process was created from real world experience and involves answering a few questions to have a better understanding of the board member's current beliefs, responses, and behaviors. The results show both you and the NPO where you are starting from, what strengths you can improve on and potential obstacles you'll need to overcome. This assessment is not about true or false answers, but provides a snapshot of the person's opportunities and potential value and helps the NPO understand the person's starting view point. You can bring a ton of value if the NPO knows how to utilize your talents properly and help you make adjustments to their process.

Goals

We hear so much about goals these days yet the numbers still show that most people do not establish or write down their goals. Mark McCormack's book, <u>What They Don't Teach You In The Harvard Business School</u>, tells of the famous Harvard study conducted between 1979 and 1989. The finding of the study (and often used statistic) was that 3% of graduates who had clear, written goals when they left Harvard were earning, on average, *ten times* as much as the other 97% of graduates *all together*. The 3% number has probably increased to 10 or 15% over the last 20 years, but is still lower than expected. The point is that if you do not understand your own goals than you'll probably not have or be able to fulfill the fundraising goals of the NPO. Your NPO must establish a fundraising goal for each board member at the start of the year, customized to each of person's skills, talents, and opportunities. If they do not set a goal for each member or they do a minimum requirement you must suggest that they take this step immediately. In fact, in our book <u>How Good Nonprofit Officers Become Great Fundraisers</u>, we discuss in detail the ASCEND process for identifying and creating your life vision. The purpose of this tool is to match the NPO executives' personal goals to the organization's mission. We've included Step 4 (5 Total Steps) of the process below showing an example of how to fill in the answers. The more clear your own goals are then the more likely you can match the NPO's goals and help them reach new heights of fundraising.

STEP 4 Evaluate: Categorize Your Goals

Example

Major Goal #1:	*Raise $5,000 for NPO this year*
Key people that are part of it:	*Bob, Jane, Chamber of Commerce*
What could stop me from achieving it?	*Not asking them in a timely manor*
If I achieved it how would people it impact my role?	*I could help 100 more or 1000 more kids if I hit this funding goal*

Beliefs

Wayne Dyer describes beliefs as, "A belief system is nothing more than a thought you've thought over and over again. It's just a repeated thought, like a habit is a repeated piece of behavior." Your belief system controls the way you interact with potential donors, sponsors, partners, and resource providers. Your current beliefs could be holding back your contribution and the current state of the economy along with underlying issues in the NPO world create easy opportunities to create new excuses. In fact, many board members find themselves lowering their expectations.
Some questions to consider:

- Do you accept less from donors because of the economy?
- What is controlling your attitude?
- What is holding you back?
- Do you believe you can raise the money?
- Do you hit the goals you need to hit?
- Are you meeting the people you need to meet?
- Are you bringing in the sponsorship dollars to keep your event or group moving forward?

You want the above questions to challenge you and your fundraising efforts especially if you are not contributing at your expected level. Typically our habits along with certain fears and mental baggage play a key role in how you react to each day and to each event in your life. Ask yourself if your beliefs are real or outdated. Start with clarifying your beliefs about what you do know, and then move forward to what you can control. Your beliefs should align with your NPO activities and tie into the best options for you to help.

Options for helping

Align yourself with the options that best fit you and your lifestyle. Remember that fundraising is not about the checks that you write, but the checks and resources you bring in from your efforts. As Napoleon Hill pointed out in his research, other people's efforts and money create financial success. This represents the mastermind formula that 1+1 can equal three and two plus two can equal 10. In fact, it's more than providing your own money; you need to focus on your time and the referrals, introductions, and resources that can come from your circle of influence. Furthermore, there are three specific ways to help, including finding other donors, introducing potential sponsors to the NPO, and/or introducing key relationships. Each method has its positives and negatives. Identify which one works best for you and spend your 30 minutes per week on that tactic. As you identify the methods that work best for you, your confidence and attitude will improve and alignment leads to the next strategy managing your **NPO fundraising time** in the most efficient way possible.

Key Action Step

(You Can Do This Right Now):

Force the NPO to establish fundraising goals for each board member – whether $150 or $100,000 – put them in writing and share them - create a culture of fundraising

My personal fundraising goal this year is $_____

Note: this is **not** the number you will personally write checks for, but the number you will help bring in via donors, sponsors, value added services, or in kind contributions

Tool:
Board Member Fundraising Goal Card*

* Available at HowGoodBecomeGreat.com

2. The Fundraising Time Management System

IT IS HARD TO FIND A PERSON IN THE COUNTRY WHO WOULD not admit to struggling with time management or the additional responsibilities brought on by adding more commitments. You end up caught in the NPO time trap because you do not use a time system customized for fundraising activities. In fact, according to Dan Sullivan from the Strategic Coach Program, "Most people work in a time and effort economy, where they organize their lives according to bureaucratic strategies. These strategies, for the most part, require time and effort but do not produce results." You want the limited time you have spent on the most productive tactics that bring about the best possible results.

You need a new strategy since we are all trying to do more in less time. All of your time overlaps with each category, burdening your schedule in one way or another. You'll only have 30 minutes to 1 hour per week on average (based on research) to complete your volunteer duties. The idea is to not focus on getting more time for fundraising activities, but rather utilize the limited time you have in a different fashion. Ask yourself how much time do you spend on fundraising efforts and how is that time structured? Now, track your time for one or two weeks and see how much time you spend to raise funds. The statistics say you spend about 5 minutes on this activity. The Fundraising Time Management System© was created to help avoid the NPO time trap and it includes two main tactics; blocking out fundraising time and extending your professional activities to your nonprofit duties.

Fundraising Time Block

Ralph Waldo Emerson hit the nail on the head when he said, "This *time*, like all times, is a very good one, if we but know what to do with it." The first step in the Fundraising Time Management System is to discipline yourself to block out your calendar (either computer or paper based), dedicating a 15 minute block of time each week for completing three to four key fundraising activities. This time block is just for fundraising tasks and not other board duties. Over time you'll expand from 15 minutes to 30 minutes to additional 30 minute blocks. You'll need to identify the block at the beginning of the month and then review and make adjustments at the beginning of each week. Sunday afternoon or early Friday morning is a great time to establish this block, or simply add this tactic into your normal weekly planning procedures. Additional good times are right before or after the board or committee meetings because typically you are more excited and relevant information is at top of mind. The intent is to have pre-determined tasks and get more specific results in less time which creates a habit of keeping the block at a consistent time each week.

Once you've blocked the time you'll want to write down what you anticipate working on, keeping in mind the importance of simplicity. The Fundraising Time Management System Form is a great tool for identifying these tasks, writing in bullet lists right in the specific time block. It only takes about two or three minutes to complete the form each week. For example, you might put down that you will do three e-mails, make three return phone calls or search the web for 10 minutes to uncover a new resource or a new sponsor on Friday afternoon from 3:00 to 3:15. Not only write in the activities, but confirm who you will be calling or e-mailing and which potential web searches you plan to conduct. In one month if you follow this system, you will have made 12 phone calls, 12 e-mails, and completed 40 minutes of research. Now taking this out over a year you'll find your fundraising numbers increasing by hundreds of percent. Remember that you'll typically find that one task equals three minutes of time. Lastly, customize this block to your schedule and if you have to move it, discipline yourself to keep it within that week.

Extend Your Professional Experience

Working with an NPO is your opportunity to feed two birds with one seed (alternative phrase to the abrasive Japanese proverb of hurting birds); contributing to the entity while gaining more professional experience and improving your skill levels. You have professional skills that can be expanded or developed by working as a board member. For example, if you are an investment manager you can serve on the financial committee or if you know IT and computers, then you can offer consulting, web development, IT support. Extending this attitude into fundraising activities will provide you with additional interaction, networking, relationship building, and promotional skills. This is your chance to develop new professional skills that will expand your career opportunities while at the same time help your NPO survive. In the process, you'll improve your passion for the organization; making the time commitment and fundraising duties easier.

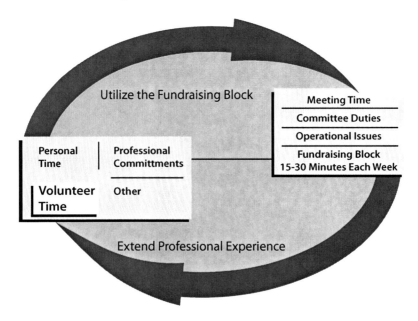

Good Time Management = More Funds Raised

Marcia Wieder said, "It's how we spend our time here and now, that really matters. If you are fed up with the way you have come to interact with time, change it." You may have great technique and skill and even lots of years of experience, but if you manage your fundraising time poorly you need to make a change. If you improve your fundraising time manage, then you are ready to tackle **Strategy 3 The Green Light Process**.

> ## Key Action Step
> *(You Can Do This Right Now):*
>
>
> Open up your computer calendar or your day timer and block out 15 minutes this week to start the process. Write down three bullet points and insert an action item for each.
>
> ### Tool:
> ### Fundraising Time Management System Form*

* Available at HowGoodBecomeGreat.com

3: The Green Light Process

IN THE MOVIE BUSINESS WHEN THEY GREEN LIGHT A PROJECT it means their moving forward into the production phase; kicking off a whirl wind of activities including signing the director, bringing on executive producers, and hiring the cinematographer. At the green light, those behind the movie believe it will be successful and their actions match their belief. As a board member you can turn on your green light when you create new money scripts, beliefs, and expectations in regards to fundraising. There is a great anonymous quote that says, "Many people think that problems with money scripts stem from ignorance about the complicated field of personal finance, and they wrongly believe that the solution lies in gathering more information, collecting more tips and strategies for budgeting and investing. This might help for some people; however, for the majority of us, a lack of information is not the problem. The basics of good financial health are actually quite simple, and more advice telling us to save more or spend less is not going to help." In the end, the mental scripts you carry around with you limit your fundraising results more than any real lack of funds, opportunities, or resources in the marketplace.

In many cases the Borrower Phenomenon© appears over and over when people have not written new mental scripts regarding asking for money or inviting a contact to attend an event. Or they are influenced by the existing scripts of the board. No matter the situation, using the tools below will help you change negative scripts into positive ones and fill in a positive experience when the last fundraising efforts left you disappointed and frustrated. It is time to turn on the Green Light.

The Money Game

From your point of view, how much money is a lot to fundraise for you? Write a number in the box – whatever comes to you first or what you feel in your gut. Now ask yourself, "Why did I put that amount in the box? It is correct?" Now ask: "Is it my true feeling or did someone or something influence the amount I put in the box?" Just by identifying this number you start to realize your first script problem.

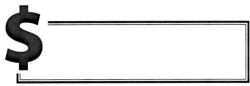

Now take the number you put in the above box and multiply it by 10.

$$ \boxed{\$ } $$

How do you feel about the new number? Not realistic? If so, why not? Start to think about what it means for the organization if you can hit this new number, evaluating all the gains, benefits, opportunities, and new clients served by reaching this new level. Now, take it another step further and have each person on the board do this exercise and then total all the member's times-10 number. You will start to create a new money script and raising the fundraising bar for the organization.

Donation Threshold

According to Boardsource, 68% of NPOs require personal contribution with the average dollar amount around $150. This low dollar amount shows that either the expectations are to low or the skill level required to raise significant funds is lacking. Board members become trapped by what they've accomplished up to today. Furthermore, all of your activities, relationships, and resources are based on the top number or the highest level of your current money script. If the number you wrote in the bottom square of the money game didn't seem real, then you're caught at your Donation Threshold Level©. You simply built your ideology around your current resource model and circle of influence. You'll need to shift your thinking in order to break through and utilize new networking tools to meet people/contacts that can bring the higher donor and sponsor value to your group and have networks where contacts provide larger donations. This change can often mean significant increases in funding levels.

The Paradigm Shift

Even though corporate and foundation giving, government grants and fees for service are down, many individuals are giving more than they ever have before. The problem is that they haven't given to your organization because they have not been asked at all or they have not been asked in a proper fashion. That is one of the key challenges in the NPO world; board members who are afraid to ask or who are not asking enough people. When you shift your paradigm by writing new scripts, your first step is to change your attitude. You must approach the process with positive energy, enthusiasm, and a willingness to change. In fact, you make your NPO responsibility top of mind, drinking the Kool-Aid as such because your 100% committed to raising your expectations. The money game helped you identify the gap between what you currently think is a significant amount of funding and the level of funding you could obtain. As you begin to make the paradigm shift you need to remember that it is about improvement over perfection.

Louise Hay, founder of Hay House Publishing and author of the book <u>You Can Heal Your Life</u>, which has sold more than 35 million copies throughout the world explains, "Your beliefs and ideas about yourself and the roles you play are often the cause of our emotional problems and physical maladies." She emphasized the importance of the words you tell yourself in your own mind. Furthermore, Saturday Night Live actor and writer, Al Franken, took a shot at self-talk via his character Stuart Smalley, "I'm good enough, I'm smart enough, and dog-gone it, people like me." The irony of the spoof was the truth in it. If your heart does not believe the words you express then you are not taking action and wasting your time. In fact, your potential donor or partners will know if your invitation is really genuine and authentic. They'll feel it in their heart when you come from a position of knowing how to properly ask and invite and doing it in a method that reflects confidence and passion. You change your behavior by shifting your paradigm and then change the way you talk to yourself.

Self Talk Basics

Self talk is more about an attitude and what you say inside your mind then what you spout out to the world. It is using phrases and words that empower you and connect your words to your beliefs while recognizing in your mind that you may need to change or reprogram. It is not pretending like things are wonderful and saying words that you truly do not feel or believe in your heart. As you change the self talk you begin to believe the words and phrases that you use and slowly change your beliefs. Your reality begins to look more like the thoughts in your mind.

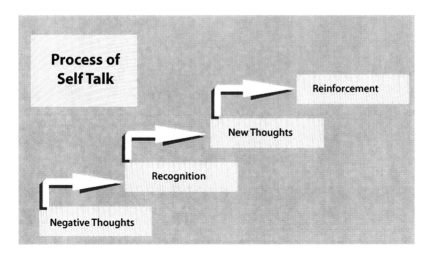

The first step is accepting that your self-talk is negative and it is based on old beliefs. Next you recognize the thoughts when they occur – i.e. "That company will not sponsor us because the economy is too tough right now." After you start to recognize the negative tones and filter the ones that no longer work for you, you create new thoughts or write new scripts. This is the point where you use daily affirmation or a gratitude journal. At the last level, you reinforce the new thoughts with consistent words, utilizing exercises on a daily basis. This includes placing the phrases where you can see them, i.e. "I am a powerful person who will gain a new major donor today," or reading from a five bullet sheet in the morning or evening (5 minute exercise).

Self Talk Options and Examples

- Silent: Sitting quietly at a coffee shop or deep meditation
- Verbalize: Out loud to yourself or others or pay close attention to the words you use
- Written: Phrasing and writing in your words or letter format, journaling, bullet points
- Video: Record yourself saying it or film yourself discussing the goal

Self-talk is an important part of your life, both personally and professionally. It can make or break you; influencing what you believe is possible or not possible on a daily basis. You'll want to pay close attention to the words you think about as well as verbalize. Remember that affirmation or positive thoughts must be in the present, specific, and cause good results. The tools you use must be simple, easy to find (daily basis), practical and realistic. Lastly, you must evaluate if the self-talk is really you and honest. Do you truly feel in your heart the words or phrases that your thinking about, writing down, or verbalizing? Is it honest?

NPO Gratitude Form

You can buy a journal off the Internet or simply contact info@billyounginspires.com to receive a form. You might have one statement that you write down each day or 3, 5, 10 statements. The quantity of gratitude statements is up to you. You can focus on just your NPO activities or incorporate both your personal and professional thoughts. Your creativity will expand as you use the tool more, evolving into statements like:

Today I am grateful for the time with my family and the presence that God plays in my life. I'm appreciative of my co-workers and clients and feel fortunate that I can sign on a new sponsor today

How You Think Matters

As you continue to write new mental scripts about money and potential success, you'll see your contribution to the NPO increase significantly. Your personal confidence will improve causing your activity to increase and your behaviors to be more in line with your beliefs. If you believe that you can raise more money you'll see green lights where before you only saw red and you can free your mind to focus on **Strategy 4 Genuine Credibility©**.

Key Action Step

(You Can Do This Right Now):

Write down one sentence in the space below that describes why you are grateful for the NPO you represent:

_____

_____

_____

**Tool:
NPO Gratitude Form***

* Available at HowGoodBecomeGreat.com

4: Genuine Credibility

IF YOU WANT TO HIT NEW FUNDRAISING LEVELS, THEN YOU have to start with the most critical strategy you can implement right now – Genuine Credibility©. Genuine Credibility© refers to having habits that others appreciate, watch, and often emulate. This means people you come in contact with on a daily basis or connect via your personal network appreciate and respect you at such a high level that their willing to do or help with anything you are passionate about. They'll move mountains for you. Indeed they believe in you to the point of wanting more success for you than do for them self. In fact, they are your cheerleader referring you to key contacts, expanding your opportunities. Also, they open up their rolodexes & databases helping make critical introductions for you and not just providing names but actually making phone calls and attending meetings with you to make sure you get connected to the right people.

Credibility increases your fundraising when you foster five key habits all built around authenticity which is defined as not false, real, and genuine. When you are authentic, you demonstrate trust and reliability through action. You have habits that are evident, consistent, and create trust. These habits cross over industry and specialty lines and have survived since the dawn of time, yet are often the most overlooked skills that one can possess. If done well you will receive more referrals, have e-mails forwarded on to thousands of contacts, and begin to see others moving mountains for you. However, if you take these habits for granted your efforts will result in frustration and disappointment. People with these habits are honest, sensitive to and tolerate other views. They are friendly, patient, and responsive, making others feel great by listening and valuing their feedback.

The Five Critical Genuine Credibility© Habits:

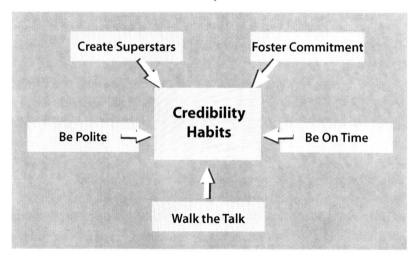

1. **Be Polite**

   Always say please and thank you no matter the situation or environment, opening doors for others, completing proper introductions, listening while others speak, apologizing if you error, and following the proper social protocol for all social interaction.

2. **Create Superstars**

   Make everyone around you look and feel important, creating opportunities for others. Don't talk negatively to other board members or volunteers about anyone for any reason.

3. **Foster Commitment**

   Finish what you started; making sure that if you commit to the goal or project, you complete it. Be sure to under promise and over deliver, surpassing expectations rather than just meeting them.

4. **Be on Time**

   Be on time (or even early) to every appointment, becoming such a fixture at events and activities that others would call 911 if you failed to show up on time.

5. **Walk the talk**

   Don't just talk about it, do it. Or in other words, go beyond talking the talk and walk the walk, leading as a role model and speaking through actions rather than just words.

These habits seem very simple and anyone with common sense should know them. However, if they are not top of mind, they become lost from our busy days filled with too much to do and not enough time to do it. When you are genuine and credible you have common decency toward others, enabling positive human connections.

Genuine Creditability© tactics separate you from the pack, enabling you to hit new and exciting levels of personal fundraising contribution and preparing you to accomplish **Strategy 5 The G² Formula**.

Key Action Step

(You Can Do This Right Now):

Write a thank you note (preferably hand written) to one person who has helped your organization, arrive 10 minutes early for your next meeting, or pick up the phone and call one Super Star supporter and just say "Thank you".

**Tool:
Genuine Credibility Habits Card***

* Available at HowGoodBecomeGreat.com

5: The G2 Formula

THE GIVE TO GET (G2) FORMULA OR PROVIDING VALUE UPFRONT before expecting value in return is a phrase thrown around, and is subsequently considered fairly cliché. It is a simple formula that speakers like Zig Zigler have emphasized in importance and even built entire methodology on the phrase, "You will get all you want in life if you help enough other people get what they want," Or in even simpler terms WIFT (What is in it for them?). We could customize this quote in the NPO world to say, "Your organization will get the donations/sponsors that you target if you help enough donors and sponsors get what they want." This formula is about giving to your donors and sponsors before they ever give anything to you.

The problem isn't that you don't know this strategy. The challenge lies in how you've forgotten it or you lack the tools to deliver it. As your organization grows and develops your own driving forces, goals and priorities become top of mind. You forget the importance of the formula. If you want to improve your fundraising efforts, simply think "give first". This goes beyond providing heart tugging stories and reduces the time you spend on asking and inviting. This formula will keep you out of the giving trap and avoid the perils of requiring instant gratification. And by giving to get you will build strong relationships that will, or could have, significant value to you in the long term. The goal is to give more value to as many people as possible before they even consider giving you and/or your organization anything.

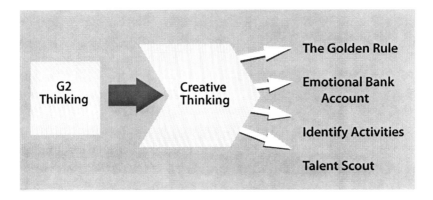

The Golden Rule

According to Wikipedia[7] "the Golden Rule is an ethical code that states one has a right to just treatment, and a responsibility to ensure justice for others." You'll also here the phrase "The ethic of reciprocity," used when describing the rule. It is arguably the most essential basis for the modern concept of human rights, though it has its critics. A key element of the golden rule is that a person attempting to live by this rule treats all people, not just members of his or her in-group, with consideration. You can apply the rule in your role as a board member or volunteer, using your knowledge and imagination. Take a few moments to understand the effect your actions have on the lives of others. Now imagine yourself in the potential donor's or sponsor's place on the receiving end of the action. It sounds so simple but is often overlooked, so remember the Golden Rule during all your interactions.

Emotional Bank Account

The Emotional Bank Account is a metaphor used to describe the give and take of most relationships and for our purposes, provides a way to build more trust in any professional relationship. There several ways to make deposits and withdraws in this set up including seeing people through their eyes and observance of the little things. As the saying goes, "little things equal big results". In fact, people typically make improper withdraws from others when they do not keep their commitment or they have different expectations. If you want others to help your NPO then make sure you are making regular deposits into the emotional bank account of your relationship, including saying thank you, sending over an articles or idea, keeping track of their kids or families lives and occurrences, or following through on any commitment you make. In the end, positive behaviors towards your prospective donors and cheerleaders results in deposits and negative behaviors become withdrawals.

Specific G2 Formula Activities

- Learn something special about each person in your network
- Find out what your potential donors care about
- Seek to understand what is important to your current and prospective donors
- Offer to do something for the donor or sponsor right at the time you learn about their priorities
- Give them ideas, resources, leads, referrals, introductions, in-kind trade
- Find one way to help them by researching their firm, personal background or hobbies
- Create new fields in your database called WIFT or personal preferences

Think like a Talent Scout

American Idol is still one of the most popular shows on TV with some 30 million people tuning in each week to see the good, the bad and the embarrassing. People also tune in to get a glimpse of the great undiscovered talents. The creators of American Idol and the four judges (or talent scouts as some might refer them) on the show have an amazing formula that can be transferred to the NPO world and by following you will be giving to your NPO before you get anything in return.

A talent scout must keep their eye on up and comers in the field, visiting sites to identify new people of interest who may not be on the scout's radar. They are often looking for specific talent. Likewise, you need to keep an open mind as you interact with others on a daily basis identifying who might benefit your NPO. As a board member you're on the lookout for the next undiscovered talent who can bring incredible value to the organization and potentially replace you either on the board or replace the amazing value you currently contribute.

In our How Good Become Great Academy, we teach the power of duplication, finding people in the market place who have great skills and similar passion to your own. There are both young and mature members of our society waiting to be recruited to make a difference. In fact, some have direct connections to the organization as either clients or family/friend of clients or have indirect ties that make them a great candidate.

What Goes Around Comes Around

When you create a culture of giving first and asking second you differentiate your organization from all the rest. In fact, you'll notice donors and sponsors coming to you rather than the other way around and this improves the chances of **Strategy 6 Think Like A Farmer** working for you.

> **Key Action Step**
> *(You Can Do This Right Now):*
>
> Write down one action you can do for someone in your network that might help them eventually bring a ton of value to your NPO

Tool:
Board Member Power of Duplication Form*

* Available at HowGoodBecomeGreat.com

strategy

6: Think Like a Farmer

IF YOU WANT TO LEARN THE FOUNDATION BEHIND NETWORKING and meeting more key people, then pay close attention to how a farmer works including their habits, attitude and tools. In many cases, your network is not weak or inefficient but your methods for approaching new people or fostering current relationships could be the problem. If you are like most people the depth of your network just doesn't exist. No matter what the reasons, there are several tools to help you overcome this situation.

Farmers don't just walk out to the fields one morning to start planting seeds and come back the next morning to harvest what they planted the day before, collecting their cash at the same time. On the contrary; they put together a strategy of how much of one seed they'll plant covering a certain acreage and then plan for additional crops taking into account the weather and ground conditions. Indeed, they buy enough to ensure that a good crop will germinate and grow until the harvest (which can be several days away). They make sure they periodically (daily) check on the growth and changes in the crops not just planting seeds and then leaving for a six month trip. They use technology and information, utilizing GPS in tractors to plant the crops, understand weather forecasts, and pricing information for when they go to market. You can expand and strengthen your network following a similar process and using all the right tools at your disposal. The key is for you to make short term sacrifices that create long term gains.

Relationships

Relationships as you know are built on trust that can take many years to establish. This trust is an integral part of gaining donor's and sponsor's help and assistance. Once you've mastered the Genuine Credibility© habits in Strategy 4 you'll need to focus on the FUEL model (Diagram follows). You'll also want to approach this like the farmer; strategy in hand, lots of patience, simple tactics, and long term thinking. This is a point where the phrase **"improvement over perfection"** should be top of mind.

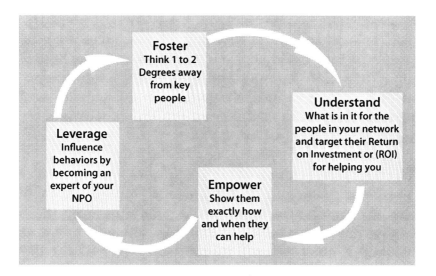

Networking Strategies and Tactics

In our Academy, we teach the four stages of relationship evolution, diving into strategies, techniques, and a proven process. For this book however, we'll briefly cover some ideas to help you strengthen and expand your network. After you understand how your fundraising goals are affected by your networking strategies, you'll want to move on to tactics.

First, start changing the way you introduce yourself at networking functions. Start with part of your NPO 60 second commercial and then lead into a story. Most people glaze over when you start off the conversation by I am an accountant, lawyer, business owner, teacher, government work, an NPO executive, etc. You can fill in any profession for the answer, but get the same psychological response. Try a new approach like, "I helped save 10,000 kids last year," or "we saved 500,000 trees last summer."

Second, take a new look at your current network. You'll need to evaluate what industries and sectors the people in your network are involved in and take note of any patterns. You may find that you're continuing to attend the same types of events with the same type of people. Ask yourself if it's time to branch out and try some new audiences.

Third, start evaluating the types of events you're attending. You can begin to see if you're in front of the right audiences and if the people attending these events have Connector Potential©. The events you're attending must attract people who can make a difference for you, move mountains, and/or impact your network. One key person with the right rolodex can expand your fundraising by $250,000 a year.

Finally, change the way you look at leads. You're building long term relationships so ask permission to put your new contacts into your fundraising process and immediately (after helping them with a priority) ask for help. If done properly you will receive one referral or introduction that can bring in significant value. How much is one new, great referral worth to you? $250,000 or more per year? $500,000 per sponsor?

Tickler Systems

Many people use some type of contact management database software; examples include ACT, saleforce.com or your company's CRM system. You have your own NPO tickler system right on your computer if you use the Microsoft operating system – called Outlook. A tickler system enables you to flag contacts for follow up with a good system helping you evaluate the time in between contacts and the methods used to engage the person (i.e. e-mail, phone call, letter, etc.).

Here is a high-level look at how an NPO tickler system works:

1. Make sure all the key people in your network are in the contacts section of outlook

2. Create a subgroup called donors and sponsors

3. Identify from your database current donors and/or sponsors as well as people you would like to invite to events or ask for specific help

4. Be sure to click on the category button and put them in the donor/sponsor category

5. Use the flag system to tickle you periodically to contact them

6. Set the flag to a date based on how you rated them (we cover ratings at our academy)

7. Briefly look at each contact and note how you can help them (you can do this in several sections of the contact file)

8. Now, after you've done something for them, utilize your 60-second NPO commercial when you reach out

The goal is to keep in touch on a basis that fits their relationship to you, their preferences, potential ability to help, and their opportunity to be a superstar for your NPO.

Increase referrals and introductions –

Increasing referrals is about establishing a habit and system that works for your style. Most people do not receive referrals because they simply do not ask. Bill Cates, author of <u>Get More Referrals Now</u>, discusses using a method to let your contacts know that you desire key introductions and you want them to help you. There are seven key tactics we teach at our academy that you can implement to increase the number of referrals you receive:

1. Give To Get: Simply and continuously give your contacts referrals, value, opportunities, gifts, etc.

2. Rewind and Remind: Let them know as often as possible and with as many different channels as possible that you live on referrals.

3. Testimonials: Help the person who is going to offer the referrals to understand why they should refer you to their contact by reminding them of either the professional or personal assistance you've offered them.

4. Create Their Circles: send over a quick bullet list of "who we'd (or I) like to meet" in an e-mail message.

5. Set the Table: Let them know how helpful it will be if they let the person know (after they've given you the name or intro) you'll be contacting them and why you'll be in touch.

6. Details Matter: Make sure you know all the details of the referral –who, what, where, when, how, etc.

7. Time Counts: Make sure you follow up immediately or within 24 hours.

Growth Takes Patience and Time

The life of a farmer can be difficult involving hard labor, digging, cutting, and worrying. The best laid plans and strategies can still be destroyed by unpredictable weather. However, if a field is prepared properly and maintained correctly, then it will produce wonderful, profitable crops. Similarly, if you prepare your networking strategies, add in consistent behavior, and foster relationships for the long term, then you will produce great results and begin **Strategy 7 Light the SPARK**.

Key Action Step

(You Can Do This Right Now):

Identify five people who could become your SUPERSTAR connectors

_____	_____
_____	_____
_____	_____

**Tool:
Board Member Tickler Form***

---

* Available at HowGoodBecomeGreat.com

strategy

7: Light the SPARK©

EVEN THOUGH BOARDSOURCE RESEARCH POINTED OUT 95% of boards' rate their fundraising as weak, board and committee meetings tend to spend 95% of their time on other issues and the lack of individualized training only exacerbates the problem. The Fundraising Fire System was created to help all the problems associated with fund-raising and includes learning an innovative 60 second commercial, a step by step process to sign on sponsors, and how to use the SPARK tool at your next meeting. These are only a few of the tools we help you implement. The entire process is simple, easy to learn and includes unique ways to say thank you and opportunities to improve professional skills while at the same time helping your NPO raise more money than ever before.

The entire board can increase contributions by utilizing the SPARK drill which when implemented correctly helps leadership ask key questions and improve the team moral while at the same time help each individual break through the knowledge ceiling. We're not talking about a raw raw session with Anthony Robbins in front of the room, although that wouldn't hurt, but a quick, outlined approach that leads to 50%, 100%, 1000% increases in fundraising activities. The challenge is to do this in a simple method that is not time consuming or disorganized. If you are part of the internal leadership or an organization that doesn't currently use a method of this nature, using this tool at your next board or committee meeting could be valuable. If you are a board member, recommend that your leadership use the tool. Of course, fundraising cannot take up all or a significant part of the meetings, but it can have impact if delivered appropriately. Anticipate about 12 to 15 minutes covering all five sections. It's time to light the first SPARK.

Utilize the SPARK drill

- Review the overall NPO Fundraising Goal & Have each board member pull out their Goal Card

- Have each member very quickly go around the table to say how close % wise they are to hitting their own personal fundraising goal

- Time - 3 minutes

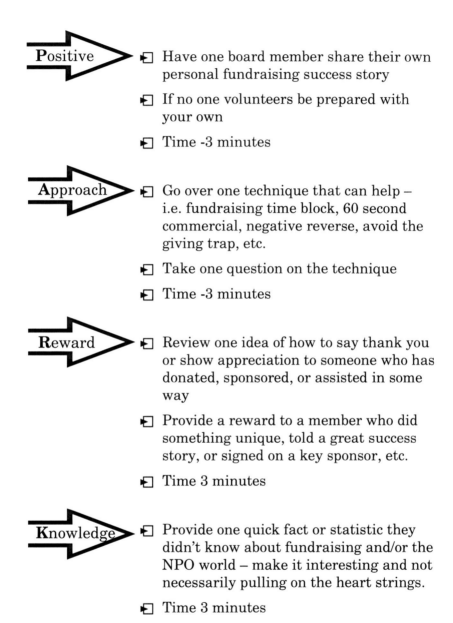

Positive
- Have one board member share their own personal fundraising success story
- If no one volunteers be prepared with your own
- Time -3 minutes

Approach
- Go over one technique that can help – i.e. fundraising time block, 60 second commercial, negative reverse, avoid the giving trap, etc.
- Take one question on the technique
- Time -3 minutes

Reward
- Review one idea of how to say thank you or show appreciation to someone who has donated, sponsored, or assisted in some way
- Provide a reward to a member who did something unique, told a great success story, or signed on a key sponsor, etc.
- Time 3 minutes

Knowledge
- Provide one quick fact or statistic they didn't know about fundraising and/or the NPO world – make it interesting and not necessarily pulling on the heart strings.
- Time 3 minutes

After this tool is implemented you will see members improve their efforts by 500% in some cases – the results will beat your expectations.

Implementing a System

There are almost as many sales, marketing, and fundraising systems as there are people attempting to use them. Our system is based off of real life experience from the trenches and incorporates a process that is simple to learn. The formula $CQ+P^3$ = Funds stands for Confidence with proper Questions plus power, presentation, and partnership can equal tremendous levels of donors and sponsorships (i.e. lots of funds). This system eliminates the need to guess at your next step or take ineffective actions.

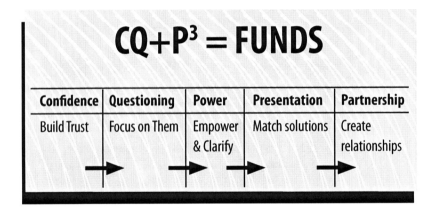

$$CQ+P^3 = FUNDS$$

Confidence	Questioning	Power	Presentation	Partnership
Build Trust	Focus on Them	Empower & Clarify	Match solutions	Create relationships

Your Confidence increases their confidence in you

C Establishing a close emotional bond with another person is an incredibly important step and can be done in seconds by having Genuine Credibility habits and mirroring or matching them. Match the speed they talk, the words they use, the way they dress, and show sincere interest in who they are and the value they bring to other's lives.

Q *Questions change the game*

You'll find that most people talk too much. In fact, it's not quantity but quality especially when you consider that the Gettysburg address was 272 words while the average conversation about your NPO is probably way too long. If you're talking then you're not fundraising. The questioning process starts with a great 60 second commercial and extends into open ended questions that keep the focus on the prospective sponsor or donor. You no longer have to ask for anything specifically, but your style and type of questions produces the right answers without confusion or drama. If you want to be different, then act different.

Example questions include (There are 12 powerful questions you can ask – four are below):

- What types of organizations do you give your time or money to?
- What do you look for in NPOs?
- How much money do you typically give each year? (Budget & Investment Questions)
- Who do you know that might want to help our group?

P³ *Yield the Power*

You need to find out how they make decisions and who else influences their choices. However, you have to keep them in the driver seat, leading this part of the process. Key question: When you've donated or sponsored in the past, how did you know you'd made a good decision?

Play the match game

If you were listening (and taking notes is highly recommended) during the Q (or Questioning) part of the formula then matching the solutions to the problems becomes easier. The prospective donor or sponsor may not care that you've been around for 100 years or that you have had the same staff for 10 years. They told you their concerns when you asked the proper questions so now match your solutions to those answers. Lastly, keep in mind that most donors' need to know immediately how you're NPO has a better ROI then another one (Differentiation point – we call it the Pink Cat)

Creating long term relationships

Partnership is defined as "a relationship between individuals or groups that is characterized by mutual cooperation and responsibility, as for the achievement of a specified goal." You're looking for something more intense than just a front line relationship. In fact, you want a partnership where you provide help and assistance and receive it back. Make sure you have a proper tickler system, identify your superstars, and focus on improvement over perfection.

Unique thank you gifts and ideas

Sponsors, donors, in-kind contributors, and resource outlets love to be thanked. In fact, you cannot thank them enough. The key is to come up with some creative ways to show your appreciation. Once again focus on what they like and what they need and gift ideas will come to you and your team in a simple fashion. A few unique ideas:

- Have a t-shirt made showing their company logo intertwined with your NPO logo (get permission of course)
- Have your clients (children) make pictures and turn them into promotional tools for the sponsor
- Do a thank you coffee meeting – invite your top 10 superstars and provide coffee and a bagel – 30 minutes just to say thanks (no event planning required).

These are just a few from our library of ideas. Spend a few minutes with your fellow board members and volunteers to brainstorm.

Ignite a Blazing Fundraising Fire

Volunteers need systems and tools not because they lack professional skills, but because they lack time and are overloaded with professional commitments. The Fundraising Fire System helps both the leadership and the board members increase fundraising levels while at the same time improve moral, create a positive culture, and grow additional community leaders. Now that you've started the SPARK go ahead and pour fuel on the fire.

Key Action Step

(You Can Do This Right Now):

What is one successful tactic you've tried this year that resulted in a fundraising opportunity for the NPO?

_____

_____

_____

_____

_____

**Tool:
Board Member SPARK Drill Form***

* Available at HowGoodBecomeGreat.com

how good become great

Ignite a Blazing Fundraising Fire

Web Site **www.HowGoodBecomeGreat.com** or **www.BillYounginspires.com**

- Lots of great tips and articles
- FREE Stuff
- Interactive Blog
- Sign up for the e-mail newsletter
- Register for a webinar or workshop
- Ask questions
- Follow us on twitter or connect on face book

Webinars & Workshops

Intro to How Good Board Members Become Great Fundraisers (Initial 60 minute webinar that expands on the book plus quarterly trainings for board members and volunteers)
Ignite a Blazing Fundraising Fire
Talus Tuesdays
Young Success (Focused on young entrepreneurs)

Other books

<u>How Good Nonprofit Officers Become Great Fundraisers – Implementing the 7 Powerful Strategies to Ignite a Blazing Fundraising Fire</u> (available at billyounginspires.com)

<u>Webplicity</u> (Available at amazon.com or bn.com)

<u>Webplicity 2.0</u> (Available at amazon.com or bn.com)

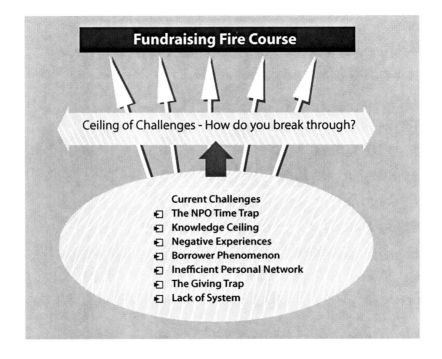

Academy

There are very few hands on, real world training courses in the country for improving your fundraising efforts. The course is unique in the industry, created for executive directors, development officers, entrepreneurs, and anyone involved in the fundraising game. Attendees can expect to learn more about fundraising in eight weeks than they have their entire life. Lastly, the tools mentioned in this book are available at the Academy or at the web site (Note: some tools are provided for free while others incorporate a fee) and include:

- SuperStars Tool
- BURN Assessment
- Goal Card
- Gratitude Form
- Tickler System
- Contribution Tracker
- SPARK Drill
- And many others

In this eight-week webinar/workshop you and your key team members will learn how to:

- Develop and maintain relationships
- Ask the right questions to identify ideal donors
- Discern what motivates people and companies to give
- Broaden your network & ask for referrals
- Explode your fundraising levels

"You read a book from beginning to end. You run a business (or Nonprofit) the opposite way. You start with the end, and then you do everything you must to reach it."

-- Harold Geneen, industrialist

CPSIA information can be obtained at www.ICGtesting.com
Printed in the USA
BVOW070348121012

302804BV00001B/67/P

9 780615 575667